W9-AES-539

NO HANDS ALLOWED
A Robbie Reader

Ronaldo

Tamra Orr

Mitchell Lane
PUBLISHERS

P.O. Box 196
Hockessin, Delaware 19707
Visit us on the web: www.mitchelllane.com
Comments? email us: mitchelllane@mitchelllane.com

Mitchell Lane PUBLISHERS

Printing   1   2   3   4   5   6   7   8   9

A Robbie Reader
No Hands Allowed

Brandi Chastain	Brian McBride	DaMarcus Beasley
David Beckham	Freddy Adu	Jay-Jay Okocha
Josh Wolff	Landon Donovan	Michael Owen
Ronaldo	Robbie & Ryan Play Indoor Soccer	

Library of Congress Cataloging-in-Publication Data
Orr, Tamara.
    Ronaldo / by Tamara Orr.
        p. cm. – (A Robbie reader. No hands allowed)
    Includes bibliographical references and index.
    ISBN 1-58415-492-6 (library bound: alk. paper)
    1. Ronaldo, 1976– –Juvenile literature. 2. Soccer players–Brazil–Biography–Juvenile literature. I. Title. II. Series.
GV942.7.R626O77 2007
796.334092–dc22
[B]
                                                                    2006014814
ISBN-10: 1-58415-492-6   ISBN-13: 9781584154921

ABOUT THE AUTHOR: Tamara Orr is a full-time writer and author living in the Pacific Northwest. She has written more than 50 educational books for children and families, including *Orlando Bloom, Ice Cube,* and *Jamie Foxx* for Mitchell Lane Publishers. She is a regular writer for more than 50 national magazines and a dozen standardized testing companies. Orr is mother to four and life partner to Joseph.

PHOTO CREDITS: Cover–AP Photo/Lionel Cironneau; p. 4–Antonio Scorza/AFP/Getty Images; p. 6–Tasso Marcelo/City Files/Globe Photos; p. 8–AP Photo/Giuseppe Calzuola; p. 11–AP/Lionel Cironneau; p. 12–AP Photo/Domenico Stinellis; p. 14–AP Photo/ Fernando Llano; p. 17–AP Photo/EFE, Mondelo; p. 18–Firo Foto/WireImage.com; p. 20–AP Photo/Jack Dabaghian; p. 23–Firo Foto/Getty Images; p. 24–Action Images/WireImage.com; p. 26–Action Images/WireImage.com

ACKNOWLEDGMENTS: The following story has been thoroughly researched, and to the best of our knowledge represents a true story. While every possible effort has been made to ensure accuracy, the publisher will not assume liability for damages caused by inaccuracies in the data, and makes no warranty on the accuracy of the information contained herein. This story has not been authorized or endorsed by Ronaldo or anyone associated with Ronaldo.

TABLE OF CONTENTS

Ronaldo (right) visits his mother, Sonia (left), his nephew Caio (lower right), and his niece Amanda. He had been training near his hometown of Rio de Janeiro, Brazil, where he had learned to play *pelada*.

Time for *Pelada!*

The young boy laughed. He had scored another goal. His friends cheered. The rag ball had just shot right into the net. Ronaldo had done it again!

Ronaldo's feet were dirty and rough from hours of playing barefoot on the streets. Playing street soccer was his favorite thing to do. He ran home from school ready to go out and meet his friends. It was time to play *pelada!*

Now and then, if his older sister was not looking, he would just skip school. Instead, he would spend the day playing ball. His mother, Dona Sonia, would be at work all day. She would

not know whether he was in class. His dad was gone. Ronaldo could not remember Nelio very well. He had left when Ronaldo was only five years old. Ronaldo had a few memories of watching his dad play soccer. His mother told him he had once played on the Portuguese

Ronaldo's son, Ronald, looks on in 2006 as his father molds his footprints for Maracanã Stadium's Walk of Fame in Rio de Janeiro. When Ronaldo was Ronald's age, he was a talented street soccer player.

team. Ronaldo was sure that wherever his dad was, he would understand why playing meant so much more to him than sitting at a school desk.

Ronaldo ran over to join his friends. Was there time for just one more game? Of course there was!

Everyone took his place in the street. Just then, Ronaldo heard his big sister Ione yell, "Dadado! It's time to come home!" He hung his head. He did not like that nickname at all. His brother Nelio had given it to him. He wished his family would stop using it.

Little did he know that one day he would have a much different nickname. Because of his speed and skill on the soccer field, his fans would call him *O **Fenômeno,*** which means "the phenomenon" (feh-NAH-meh-non) or "awesomely the best." That was a nickname he liked!

Today, though, he was just Dadado, playing street soccer and going home for dinner. Soon, all that would change.

Italian Fiorentina's Pasquale Padalino tackles the ball from Ronaldo in a semifinal match for the 1997 Cupwinners Cup. Ronaldo is playing for Barcelona, Spain. He began dreaming of playing international soccer when he was very young.

From the Neighborhood to the World

Ronaldo Luiz Nazário de Lima was born on September 22, 1976, in Rio de Janeiro (REE-oh day jeh-NAY-roh), Brazil. He took a long time to learn to how to talk. He was three years old before he started. By then, he was also following his dad around. He liked watching him play soccer. After his dad left, Ronaldo kept playing ball. He thought it was the best thing to do in the world.

When Ronaldo was only six years old, he scored a goal against his neighborhood's biggest rivals. His friends and family were very proud of him. They clapped and cheered. It

was already clear that his future would center on soccer.

By the time Ronaldo was 12, he had left street soccer behind. First, he played **futebol de salão,** or indoor soccer. Using a size two ball, he learned all the tricks of moving a very small ball with his feet.

In 1988, Ronaldo signed up with Social Ramos. He wanted to play like his hero, Zico. He thought this soccer legend was the greatest player ever. Even as an adult, Ronaldo said that Zico was the main person who had inspired him to be part of the game. Ronaldo was sure that like Zico, he too would become one of the best soccer players in the world.

At age 14, Ronaldo signed a **professional** contract with Social Ramos. For the next few years, he played for Brazil. During the 1991– 1993 season, he scored a goal in every single game he played.

He was making a lot of money. He was happy. Everybody knew who he was. It was

By June 2006, Ronaldo wasn't just playing international soccer. He was scoring goals for his Brazil team in a World Cup match against Ghana.

not long, however, until he set his sights on something even bigger. He wanted to go beyond his home country. He wanted to become an international player.

Belgium's Mbo Mpenza (left) tries to tackle the ball from Ronaldo in a 2002 World Cup soccer match between Belgium and Brazil. Brazil won the match 2-0.

Going Dutch

At the age of 17, Ronaldo left behind the world he knew and went all the way to the Netherlands. He signed with the Dutch team PSV Eindhoven. In March 1994, he became an international player. He came out on the field, full of power and passion—and still wearing braces. Soon he was their top scorer. He would dart across the field dribbling amazingly fast. Fans were watching his every move. So were scouts from other teams. People began calling him Ronaldinho, or "Little Ronaldo," since there was another player on the Brazil team with the same name. (A few years later, he would be

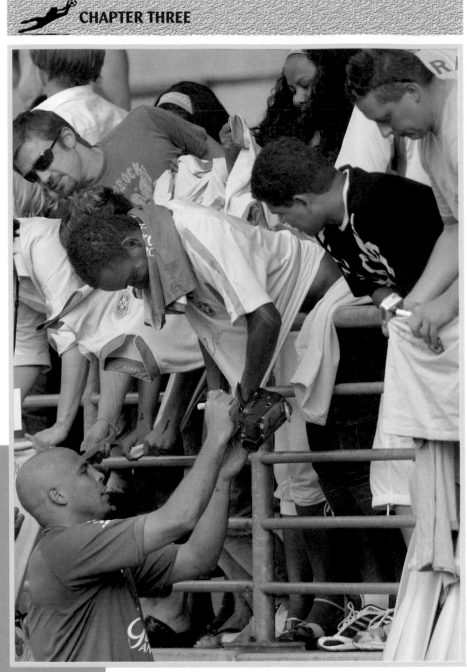

Brazil fans eagerly wait for Ronaldo to sign their team jerseys. Later that week, Brazil would face France in the 2006 World Cup quarterfinal match. The first time his team reached the World Cup, when he played for PSV Eindhoven in 1994, Ronaldo had to watch from the bench.

known again as Ronaldo, and another Brazilian player would take the name Ronaldinho.)

Ronaldo was happy with his career as a **striker.** He remembered what his life had been like as a small child. He said, "When I was growing up as a boy in Rio, I had plenty of dreams about where I wanted my football career to go. I had many dreams but I never dreamt it would happen as quickly as it did. Each goal I score is like a message of encouragement to the poor."

In 1994, PSV Eindhoven won the World Cup. Ronaldo's coach had him spend the entire time sitting on the bench. Fans were upset. They wanted to see him out on the field. If he had been allowed to play, he would have been one of the only two 17-year-olds in

the world to win the World Cup. (The other one was Pelé.)

In 1996, Ronaldo signed up with Spain's Barcelona. He did great there, too. He scored 34 goals in 37 games. He made so many goals that some defenders did not even try to stop him once he was past the **midfield line.**

Soon, Ronaldo felt the need to move on again. This time he signed up with Italy's Inter Milan. More than 10,000 people would show up just to watch him practice. Soccer fans all over the world adored him. He was winning awards. He was considered one of the best players in history. It seemed he could do no wrong out on the field.

It would not last. Ronaldo was headed for trouble. Nobody knew it. Not even him!

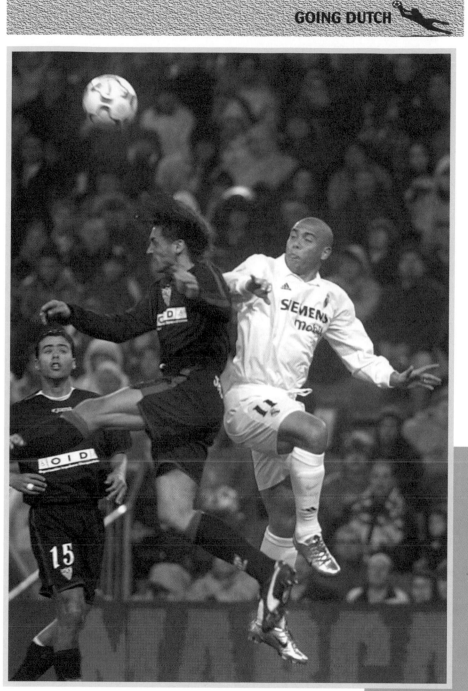

Seville's Javi Navarro beats Ronaldo (right) to a high ball during a 2003 Spanish league soccer match between Seville and Real Madrid. Ronaldo would play on two teams for Spain: with Barcelona in 1996 and, years later, with Real Madrid.

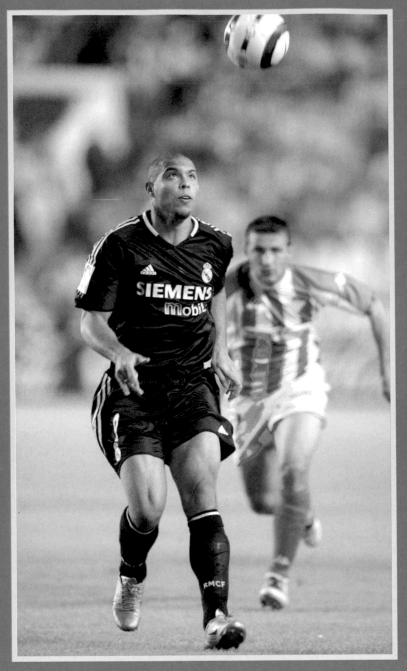

Ronaldo waits for a pass in a 2004 Spanish league match between Betis and Real Madrid. Ronaldo and his fans never gave up hope that he would play again after suffering a serious knee injury in 1999.

Years of Trouble

So far, everything had gone great for Ronaldo. The next four years would be different. They would be hard ones for both him and his fans.

Hours before the 1998 World Cup final, Ronaldo got sick and was rushed to the hospital. The doctors could not find anything wrong with him. They let him go. To everyone's surprise, he played in the game. He did not play well, though, and his team lost.

A year later, while out on the field, he hurt his right knee very badly. He tore the **ligaments** (LIH-gah-mintz) in it. Doctors

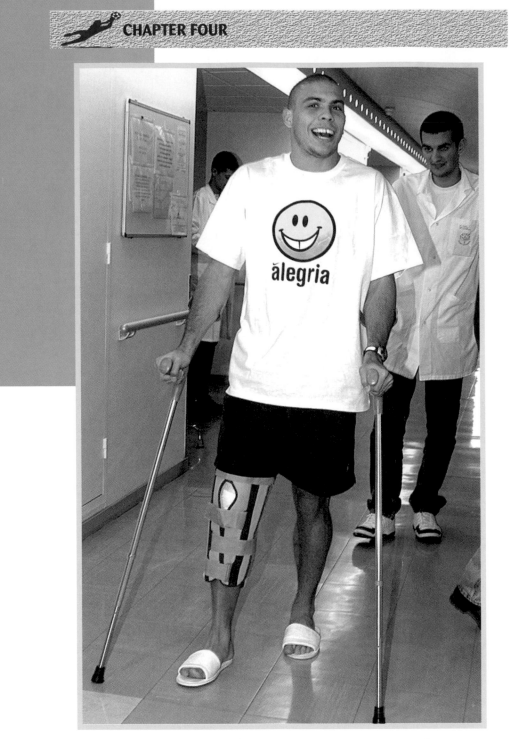

In December 1999, after having surgery to repair torn ligaments in his right knee, Ronaldo hoped for a quick recovery.

worked hard to fix it. He could not play for months. He stayed at home recovering with his new wife, Milene Domingues.

Ronaldo came back to the game in 2000. He was playing in the Italian Cup final. Fans held their breath. Was their hero back at last? Just seven minutes into the game, they found out. Ronaldo hurt the same knee again. He was down!

He had to have two operations. Then he needed two years of care before he was able to play again. It was a long wait. His fans did not forget about him, though. To honor him, they called out his name whenever his team played. It was their way of saying they missed him. They wanted him to hurry up and come back! Ronaldo wanted the very same thing.

Ronaldo had made it through the rough times. Now he had to get back out in the game and make himself and his fans happy. Could he do it? Of course! Some amazing goals were waiting, as well as some big changes.

Ronaldo announces he has signed with Real Madrid in September 2002. He made his comeback with a splash: His contract with Real Madrid was worth $45 million.

Making a Comeback

At last, Ronaldo's leg was better. It was time for him to join his team out on the field again. He wowed the crowd by scoring two goals against Germany in the 2002 World Cup. He was their top scorer! He said, "My big victory, as I have said, was to play football again, to run again and to score goals again."

By late summer, Ronaldo knew it was time to sign up with a different team. He was not getting along well with his coach. In July 2002, he joined Real Madrid. At the signing, **vendors** were selling a T-shirt with his name on it. The sales broke every record. Everyone seemed to

Ronaldo outmaneuvers Ghana's Sulley Ali Muntari during an early match in the 2006 World Cup. Brazil defeated Ghana 3-0. Brazil would move up to meet France in the quarterfinal.

want one. His fans had clearly missed their number one player.

It was the end of the year before Ronaldo got the chance to play. When he walked out on the field, he scored a goal against Brescia. Next, he scored two against Verona. Ronaldo was surprised to see the other teams' fans clapping for him. It was a kind thing to do. It showed that the whole soccer world was behind him. He appreciated the support, especially as he went through a divorce from Domingues in 2003.

In June 2004, this speedy striker scored a **hat trick** for Brazil. The game was against longtime rival Argentina, and it was a qualifying game for the 2006 World Cup. Ronaldo made all three of Brazil's goals with penalty kicks!

The following year, Ronaldo stayed with Real Madrid. He married and divorced Brazilian model Daniella Cicarelli. He was also named a Goodwill Ambassador of the United National Development Programme. As ambassador, he and fellow soccer star Zidane donated

Ronaldo and Lilian Thuram of France (15) battle for possession of the ball in a 2006 World Cup quarterfinal match. France won the match 1-0, eliminating Brazil from the competition.

$120,000 for school materials and supplies for thousands of children living in Haiti.

Ronaldo's days of playing rag ball barefoot in the street are long over now. The lessons he learned there helped earn him his worldwide fame. Ronaldo has been a terrific player since he was young. There is no doubt that he will keep amazing his fans for many years to come.

1976 Ronaldo Luis Nazário de Lima is born in Rio de Janeiro, Brazil, on September 22.

1982 He scores a goal against neighborhood rivals.

1988 Ronaldo signs with Social Ramos.

1990 He signs a professional contract with Social Ramos.

1991 He begins playing for Brazil and stays two years.

1994 Ronaldo signs with PSV Eindhoven/ Dutch; his team wins the World Cup.

1996 He signs with Barcelona/Spain; is awarded FIFA World Footballer of the Year; his team wins the Dutch Cup.

1997 He signs with Inter Milan/Italy. He is named European Footballer of the Year and FIFA World Footballer of the Year.

1998 His playing is hampered by undetermined health problems. He plays poorly in the World Cup.

1999   He severely injures his right knee and is out for several months. He marries Milene Domingues.

2000   He reinjures knee after only a few minutes of playing in Italian Cup final; son Ronald is born April 6.

2002   He signs with Real Madrid for $45 million; is named European Footballer of the Year and FIFA World Player of the Year; wins World Cup and is top scorer (8 goals); wins Golden Boot award; wins Intercontinental Cup and European Super Cup.

2003   His team wins the Spanish Super Cup. In September, he and Milene divorce.

2004   He scores a hat trick for Brazil.

2005   He marries and divorces Daniella Cicarelli.

2006   His goal helps secure Brazil a 1-0 victory over Russia in a friendly game. Brazil makes it to the World Cup quarterfinals but is eliminated by France.

fenômeno　　　(fee-NOH-mee-noh)—Portuguese for *phenomenon,* something or someone who is exceptional.

futebol de salão　　(FOOT-bol deh sah-LAH-oh)—Portuguese for *indoor soccer.*

hat trick　　　Scoring three or more goals by the same player in a game.

ligaments　　　(LIH-gah-mintz)—The tissues that connect bones.

midfield line　　The line that is halfway between goals.

pelada　　　　(peh-LAH-dah)—Portuguese for *street soccer.*

professional　　(pruh-FEH-shuh-nul)—Someone who is paid to play a sport.

striker　　　　(STRY-kur)—A forward whose main responsibility is to score goals.

vendors　　　(VEN-durs)—People who sell things, especially those who sell from market stalls.

FIND OUT MORE

Books

While there are no other books on Ronaldo, you might enjoy reading the following soccer books from Mitchell Lane Publishers:

Brandi Chastain	*Brian McBride*
DaMarcus Beasley	*David Beckham*
Freddy Adu	*Jay-Jay Okocha*
Josh Wolff	*Landon Donovan*
Michael Owen	

Works Consulted

"All I Want Is Ronaldo."
http://alliwantisronaldo.free.fr/history/history/php

Jensen, Peter. "Ronaldo Weighing Heavily on the Mind of Real During Troubled Times." [London] *Times* Online, March 7, 2006.
http://www.timesonline.co.uk/article/0,,3361-2072838,00.html

Lawrence, Amy. "Ronaldo's Resurgence Faces Its Ultimate Challenge." [London] *Observer,* June 30, 2002, http://observer.guardian.co.uk/worldcup2002/story/0,11031,746623,00.html

Mahoney, Ridge. "Persistent Pressure Just a Part of Being Ronaldo." *USA Today,* July 26, 2005.
http://usatoday.com/sports/soccer/world/2005-07-26-ronaldo_x.htm?csp=34

"Ronaldo," *World Soccer,* February 9, 2003.
http://www.worldsoccer.com/interviews/

ronaldo_interview_55866.html

"Ronaldo's Steps to Stardom." http://news.bbc.co.uk/
sportsacademy/hi/sa/football/features/
newis_2587000/2587283.stm

"Top That." *Al-Ahram Weekly,* July 4–10, 2002.
http://weekly.ahram.org.eg/2002/593/sp2.htm

United Nations Development Programme. "School Kits
for 4,300 Disadvantaged Children Paid For by
Ronaldo and Zidane," October 25, 2005.
http://content.undp.org/go/newsroom/haiti-ronaldo-
zidane251005.en?categoryID=349435&g11n.enc=ISO-
8859-1&lang=en

Wahl, Grant. "Seize the Day." *Sports Illustrated.com,*
July 2, 2003, http://sportsillustrated.cnn.com/
si_online/news/2002/07/02/seize_the_day

World Soccer. "Ronaldo." (interview)
http://www.worldsoccer.com/interviews/
ronaldo_interview_55866.html

Web Addresses

Brazilian Soccer Schools, United States
http://www.icfds.com/unitedstates/

ESPN Soccernet: Luiz Ronaldo
http://worldcup.espnsoccernet.com/
player?id=20123&lang=en

Expert Football Profile
http://www.expertfootball.com/players/ronaldo/
index.php

INDEX